the
HEINZ
ketchup
bottle

marcel verhaaf

copyright

BIS Publishers
Building Het Sieraad
Postjesweg 1
1057 DT Amsterdam
The Netherlands

T +31 (0)20 515 02 30
F +31 (0)20 515 02 39

bis@bispublishers.nl
www.bispublishers.nl

ISBN 978-90-6369-230-8

Copyright © 2011
Marcel Verhaaf
and BIS Publishers

Design Marcel Verhaaf
and Paulien Hassink
www.phontwerp.nl

contents

packaging icons
marcel verhaaf

The word 'iconic' nowadays is used in many different ways. It is often used to replace a word like famous. Some complain it is overused in attempts to stress the importance of the subject, thus losing its initial meaning.

A true icon should be more: a visual representation which triggers the instant recognition of its underlying significance for a wide group of people. I am not in favour of trying to formulate a perfectly precise definition. First, I think this is outside the scope of my objectives. Second, I would like to avoid the idea of a strict definition as the only objective and absolute criterion. As has been said before, something becomes an icon when it is seen that way by its own specific audience. People, artworks and buildings can be iconic, but so can products, or something that has such low inherent value as packaging.

Iconic products can be part of their consumer's personal identity (self-image). They can affirm a certain attitude, wealth or membership in a cultural peer group. In all cases, they are seen as 'the real thing'. Moreover, they are products we like to be seen with. In the field of packaging, there is quite a difference between famous and iconic. Becoming famous or well known may be simply a matter of repetition, supported effectively by smart, widespread advertising. Or by a strong sales and distribution programme, realizing as many product encounters as possible at various points of purchase. For me, iconic packaging is much more than that.

In my view, packaging that lacks authenticity can never become iconic, whether it is famous or not. To become authentic, a design at least has to be unique. And it also has to retain the basic outline of this unique design over a long period of time. The classic comparison of Coca Cola and Pepsi packaging is the best way to illustrate this. The Coca Cola logo and bottle design has kept its recognizable shape over almost 100 years. Its main competitor has introduced different designs and logos every few years. With no disrespect to the quality of Pepsi's current design, it is not iconic at this time.
On its own, a unique design is not enough either. It only becomes iconic after a substantial number of products have been sold, accumulating enough communicative substance to be seen as successful. Success is a property that consumers like to be associated with.

MOST ICONIC PACKAGES HAVE ONE THING IN COMMON: THE LACK OF A PRODUCT VISUAL.

Like all iconic images, they are above all the triggers to their underlying significance. They act self-assured and avoid trying too hard to convince consumers based on something as crass as the product's benefits. To become part of my personal pack- aging 'hall of fame', a package has to meet some additional criteria.

First, the combination of 3D design and 2D design needs to be directly associated with a specific product. To illustrate: a white cardboard bucket is only recognized as a container. An image of Colonel Sanders will be easily recognized as representing the Kentucky Fried Chicken brand. It is only after this image is applied to the bucket that we see the world's most iconic fried chicken packaging. The shape of the Heinz label is iconic for the brand, but it's also used for most of their other products. When it's applied to the octagonal bottle, it is recognized as Heinz ketchup right away. Even when no logo or text is visible in the label, we still recognize the product as such. Second, the packaging should be commercially

available in a format that is essentially still the same as it has been over time. Since 1887, Maggi sauce has been recognized by its tapered square brown bottle with a long, thin neck and yellow label, and it can still be described that way.

Besides authenticity, contemporary relevance is needed to guarantee a successful future. Obviously, many products have disappeared over the years simply because the products stopped fulfilling the changing needs of consumers. Iconic packaging by itself wouldn't have saved them.

But when competing against products that offer similar relevant benefits, being iconic can give a product a competitive edge. The achieved status becomes an emotional benefit instead of a product benefit.

My goal with this book is to show the development of one of the most iconic packs around the world, and to show aspects closely related to the packaging that have contributed to the process of creating a true icon.

I will refrain from expressing my opinions on which aspects were most important; I would like to invite the reader to judge for himself, as I did.

H.J.HEINZ COMPANY

PURE FOOD PRODUCTS
HEINZ
57 VARIETIES 57

1869

THE HOUSE IN WHICH WE BEGAN.

Main Plant and
General Offices: PITTSBURGH, U.S.A.

This postcard shows us the
main plant and offices in
Pittsburgh. At the time, it
was common practice to
communicate the success
of a company by showing
the size of the factory on
letterheads and promotional
items. Heinz hasn't forgotten
its roots, though, as is
shown in the right corner,
where we can see 'the house
in which we began'.

how it all began

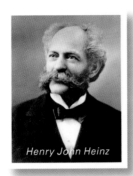

Henry John Heinz

IN MOST COUNTRIES, THE HEINZ BRAND IS NEARLY SYNONYMOUS WITH KETCHUP. IT IS NOT SURPRISING, CONSIDERING THE SUCCESS THE PRODUCT HAS HAD FOR MANY YEARS. CONSISTENCY IS ONE OF THE KEY FACTORS THAT HAS MADE THIS PRODUCT A WORLDWIDE ICON.

The company has had a consistent vision for the purity and quality of their products, as well as the importance of advertising, marketing and sales. The result has been one of the world's most famous packaging icons, the octagonal ketchup bottle. Very few companies can compete with Heinz on the consistency of their packaging design.

Heinz & Noble was officially founded in 1869. In that year, Henry J. Heinz and his neighbour L. Clarence Noble started producing and selling bottled food products under the Anchor label. Their company operated out of the original Heinz family home on Main Street in Sharpsburg, Pennsylvania.

Henry John Heinz's career in the food business started long before that date. At a very young age, he helped his mother by selling the garden's surplus, in which he proved himself to be very successful. With the help of his mother, he began to sell her bottled horseradish. This was quite a popular product at the time. Generally, horseradish was sold in coloured glass bottles, obscuring cheap fillers which were often added, like turnips, grape leaves, or sawdust. To show the purity of his mother's product, Henry offered it in clear glass. This packaging innovation became one of the cornerstones of the company.

The 1873 economic depression did not slow down the growth of the company. By 1875, it had become a major purveyor of processed condiments and sauces. The range included celery sauce,

Tomatoes transported by horse and wagon

pickled cucumbers, sauerkraut and vinegar. In only six years, the production had increased to 15,000 barrels of pickles and 50,000 barrels of vinegar a year. Unexpectedly, 1875 would reveal itself as a catastrophic year.

In April 1875, the company's lack of capital was depressing the normally hyperactive Henry. The company's economic circumstances would remain miserable over the next months. The death blow was finally dealt by phenomenal harvests which had to be purchased at high prices, due to pre-harvest price agreements. After applying for additional funds to cover purchases and wages, the company officially went bankrupt on December 17th of that year.

In 1876, the new F&J Heinz company was launched by Henry J. Heinz, his brother John and their cousin Frederick. That same year, an important new product was added to their assortment: catsup. Later written as 'ketchup', the new addition was made according to the same standards of purity and quality. The success of this product, and of course Henry's business acumen, made the company prosper for many years that followed.

Tomato sorting tables

1886 would mark the beginning of Heinz's interest in foreign markets. That year, Henry and his family travelled to Europe for the first time. He became very excited about the English, travelling to Europe almost every year between 1890 and 1914. The very well established Fortnum and Mason, purveyors for the British royal family, became the first international customer. Henry was apparently very convincing; they immediately ordered the whole range of condiments. Later, Heinz established sales branches in the United Kingdom and Canada, becoming the first US company to expand internationally.

The company grew steadily over the next few years, making good use of such modern innovations as automobiles, refrigerators and tank cars. A range of impressive advertising and marketing ideas materialized under the personal direction of the company's founder. One of the most striking was New York City's first large electric display, with 1200 incandescent light bulbs. Adding to the huge commercial success of the 12 factories in the US and abroad, Henry became a man of mythical proportions, credited for revolutionizing food processing, marketing and public eating habits.

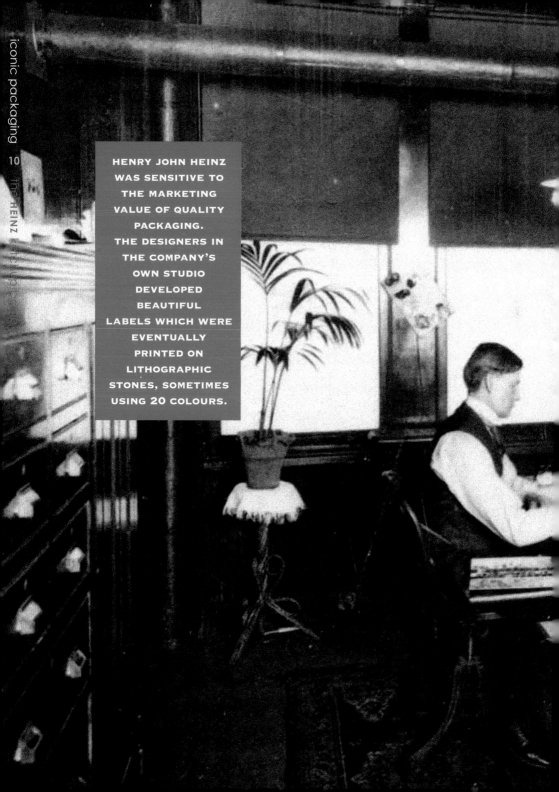

HENRY JOHN HEINZ
WAS SENSITIVE TO
THE MARKETING
VALUE OF QUALITY
PACKAGING.
THE DESIGNERS IN
THE COMPANY'S
OWN STUDIO
DEVELOPED
BEAUTIFUL
LABELS WHICH WERE
EVENTUALLY
PRINTED ON
LITHOGRAPHIC
STONES, SOMETIMES
USING 20 COLOURS.

Filling ketchup bottles, labelling, washing and wrapping

HOWARD POURED MONEY INTO PRINT ADS AND RADIO COMMERCIALS

When Henry's son Howard came to work full-time for the company in 1900, he started challenging Henry's distrust of scientists, chemists and college graduates.

The company hired its own bacteriologists in 1912, leading to the introduction of scientific methods of processing, preservation and production, all monitored from 'the quality control department'.

The prosperous 1920s were booming for the business. The company oversaw 150,000 acres of farmland, 25 factories, 116 pickle-salting plants, 755 railroad cars owned or operated by the company, 1337 representatives, as well as various seed farms and plant nurseries in greenhouses. Howard managed to control it all by giving significant autonomy to a limited number of highly talented managers in each country. During that decade, he dug the company out of debt in a time when most companies were taking out loan after loan. This financial prudence paid off during the Great Depression of the 1930s. In contrast to many other companies, Heinz invested in more new products and more advertising. From 1933 on, the company's sales started increasing again. Howard subsequently invested in print advertising, radio commercials and market research.

When Howard died of a stroke at the age of 64, he left a huge organization to Henry John Heinz II (known as Jack to his friends). The company and its 17,000 employees were facing immense wartime challenges. Rationing and food import restrictions caused the number of varieties to decline. A wartime ban on tin for civilian uses cut out 23 varieties of soup, causing 1000 employees to lose their jobs. To save valuable metals, baked beans were sold in glass jars. Whenever possible, baby food was packaged in paper containers. In the end, the idle factory machinery and work capacity were used to produce parts for military airplanes.

THOUSANDS OF
FAMILY-RUN
GROCERY STORES
WERE BEING
SUPPLANTED BY
FEWER, LARGER
STORES AND
SUPERMARKET
CHAINS.

<u>1957</u>

To fund Jack's ambitious post-war plans, the company floated its first public stock in September 1946. Between 1945 and 1965, the company expanded and appeared to be prospering; its products were sold in over 200 countries. In the United Kingdom, Heinz products did so well that many British consumers believed Heinz to be an English company. The soaring profits at Heinz UK contributed hugely to the company, compensating for the decreasing profits in the United States.

In the US, the small, family-run grocery stores were being supplanted by larger stores and supermarket chains. To anticipate the changing situation, most food companies were becoming more marketing-driven. However, Heinz USA was sluggish to adapt to this new reality. Its philosophy was that only volume produced profit, a principle that ate into the company's ability to respond to changing markets. Soup, baby food, ketchup and pickles were losing market share to competitors. A change in management and Jack's move to non-executive chairman made it time for a transformation.

1966

In 1966, Burt Cookin became president and CEO of the H.J. Heinz Company. His policies made Heinz a driving competitor in the food business again. He transformed the paternalistic family firm into a thoroughly professional company, essentially shaping the company into its modern form.

His successor, Anthony J.F. O'Reilly, is credited with transforming the H.J. Heinz Company into a global player.

O'Reilly was responsible for the acquisition of Weight Watchers International for 100 million US dollars, accurately anticipating the upcoming consumer obsession with health, wellness and fitness. He became president and CEO of the company in July 1979.

BUILDING ON THE FOUNDATION OF THE COMPANY THAT COOKIN HAD MODERNIZED AND PROFESSIONALIZED, O'REILLY BUILT A COMPANY THAT BECAME ONE OF THE PREMIER STARS IN THE FIRMAMENT OF THE FOOD SECTOR.

1882-1905
*The 'handsome
bottle'*

TOMATO CATSUP, (8 oz.)

catsup or ketchup?

FOR A VERY LONG TIME, BOTH SPELLINGS WERE USED SIDE BY SIDE. THE WORD 'CATSUP' DATES BACK THOUSANDS OF YEARS TO A SAUCE USED IN ASIA.

Most sources cite ke-tsiap (a Chinese word) as the oldest name. In its original form, ke-tsiap was more like a traditional soy sauce. Common ingredients included kidney beans, anchovies, walnuts and mushrooms. The product made its way to Malaysia and Indonesia, where it was known respectively as kechap or ketjap. In the 17th century, British and Dutch sailors brought it to the West and called it 'catchup'. The first account of tomatoes being added to the mixture is from that period. Sandy Addison is credited with creating one of the first tomato ketchup recipes in 1801. Various similar recipes popped up in cookbooks in the first three decades of the 19th century. By 1837, ketchup was sold throughout the USA, thanks to the efforts of Jonas Yerkes. Among other ingredients, his recipe included tomato pulp, green tomatoes and lots of sugar and vinegar. The product's huge success started when the tomato ketchup made by the H.J. Heinz Company debuted at the Philadelphia Fair in 1872. Heinz later introduced its tomato ketchup in 1876 as one of the first products sold under the F+J Heinz Co. name.

In the second half of the twentieth century, the market was dominated by three major players, all of which were using different names for their tomato ketchup: Heinz Ketchup, Del Monte Catsup and Hunt's. Hunt's even used three: Hunt's Catsup (east of the Mississippi), Hunt's Ketchup (west of the Mississippi) and Hunt's Cornchops (in Iowa). Millions of dollars were spent by all three companies to control ownership of whichever spelling won out. Over time, the majority opted for 'ketchup'. The battle between ketchupers and catsupers came to an end in the 1980s, when ketchup was officially declared a vegetable on the US government's standards for school lunch menus. Since catsup did not appear on the list, Del Monte finally had to change its product name to ketchup too.

1892

1889

1892

1903

1908

1889

1948   1960   2000   2008

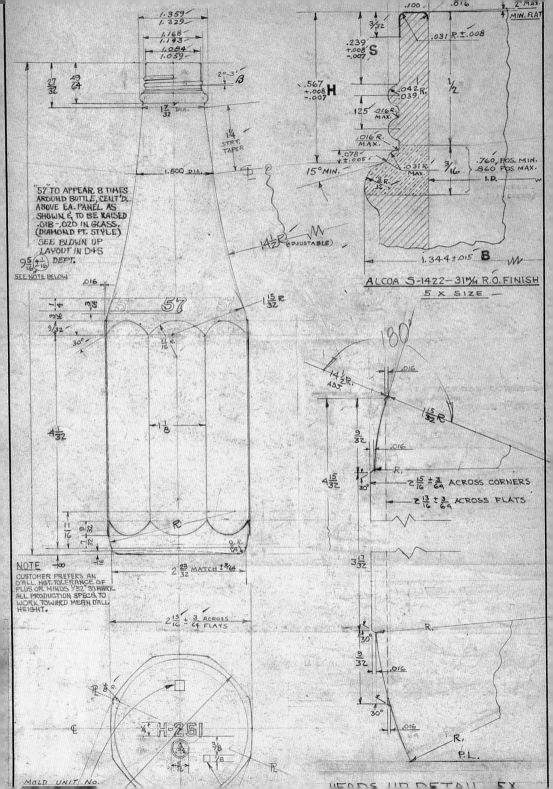

the octagonal bottle

ALL HEINZ GLASS CONTAINER VARIANTS HAD A SPECIFIC NUMBER EMBOSSED ON THE BOTTOM.

Apart from some hassle involved in getting the first dollop out of the bottle, the curved neck allows the product to flow out in a smooth and 'restrained' way. The relatively narrow mouth was chosen to expose as little as possible of the product to the air. A wider neck and mouth were tried, but rejected by consumers, because the ketchup turned dark brown faster, and the discolouration went deeper.

Henry J. Heinz applied for the patent on May 20, 1890 with the following text: 'Be it known that I, Henry J. Heinz, a citizen of the United States residing in Pittsburg, Pa., have invented and produced a new original design for a bottle. This design is a design for a flat panel bottle that has the panels extending from the bottom of the bottle to about its middle and having their side edges vertical and parallel and the converging edges or sides tapering inward from the upper end of the flat panels.'

THE FIRST OCTAGONAL BOTTLES CAN BE IDENTIFIED BY THE NUMBER 56 AND 63. THIS DESIGN WAS PATENTED ON JUNE 17, 1890

the keystone

THE ICONIC
KEYSTONE SHAPE
FIRST APPEARED IN
THE TRADEMARK
OF THE F&J HEINZ
COMPANY IN 1876.

Most likely, this symbol was chosen because Pennsylvania was known as the Keystone State. A keystone is the major stone in a foundation, and Pennsylvania was considered the central state among the USA's original thirteen colonies. The Heinz trademark shows both a keystone and a key. The key was almost certainly added by H.J. Heinz for esthetical reasons.

On the first trademarked design, the brand name was spelled Heinz's. The board decided to drop the 's' from Heinz in 1897. The town was spelled Pittsburgh when it was incorporated as a borough in 1794. In an attempt to standardize the nation's spelling of towns and cities, the U.S. Geographic Board ruled the 'h' to be deleted in 1891. In a response to protests from many Pittsburgh residents who objected to the change, the 'h' was officially restored in 1911.

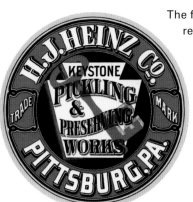

The first ketchup label with a shape related to the keystone appeared in 1876. Around 1889, a label was introduced that essentially had the same shape as the ones still in use on all current Heinz products.

1876-1885
The 'Keystone bottle'

THE ROOTS OF
THE ICONIC HEINZ
KETCHUP BOTTLE
DATE BACK TO
THIS DESIGN

first varieties

THE OCTAGONAL
BOTTLE OF 1890,
THE KEYSTONE-
SHAPED LABEL
AND THE TWO
DISTINCTIVE
HORIZONTAL BLACK
BANNERS.

These key elements have been in the minds of millions of consumers for many years. This single design has been used for several variants. Both 'Keystone ketchup' and 'tomato ketchup' were very similar to the variety that is available today. 'Home-made ketchup' had a very different recipe which used more vinegar; it was mainly used for cooking, for example stews. The variety called 'octagonal ketchup' had a thicker consistency. The design with the two black banners remained in use until 1905. Over the years, only the curly ornaments were removed from the labels.

KEYSTONE KETCHUP (12 oz. Octagon Style)

The original octagonal bottles were closed with both a metal screw cap and a cork. The metal caps were not airtight, so the use of corks helped to keep oxygen out of the product.

-from vine to glass

within an hour!

PRIZE tomatoes, red ripe; choice spices and pure sugar—skilfully blended, cooked to perfection and bottled—*all within an hour after the tomatoes come from the vines.*

That's the secret of the purity and quality and delicious flavor of MONARCH Catsup and Chili Sauce.

Other MONARCH QUALITY Food Products

Coffee	Prepared Mustard	Sweet Peas
Tea	Salad Mustard	Telephone Peas
Cocoa	Pork and Beans	Extra Small Sifted
Teenie Weenie	Prepared	Early June Peas
Sweet Pickles	Spaghetti	Spinach
Sweet Relish	Yankee Beans	Red Kidney Beans
Sweet Chow	Cherries	Stringless Beans
Mayonnaise	Cling Peaches	Lima Beans
Thousand Island	Fruit Salad	Asparagus Tips
Dressing	Pineapple	Tomatoes
Teenie Weenie	Golden Bantam	Salmon
Peanut Butter	Corn	Sardines

MONARCH
Quality for 70 years
REID, MURDOCH & CO.

Established 1853
General Offices, Chicago, U.S.A.
Branches: Boston · Pittsburgh · New York

Our Monarch Quality Food Products are sold only by Independent Retail Grocers who own and operate their own stores

© 1926, R. M. & Co.

inspired competition

MOST CATEGORIES OF FOOD PRODUCTS SOLD IN STORES HAVE A VERY SPECIFIC AND RECOGNIZABLE VISUAL LANGUAGE. The development of a specific visual language usually takes many decades. In fact, you could compare such a development with Darwin's theory of evolution. After many years of competition, only the fittest will survive. In the field of packaging, we can see the consumer's image of an overall category being determined by the most successful examples. In most cases, competitors will follow the design of the market leaders – sometimes simply because it is the easiest way to grab a piece of the pie. Generally, after a while, consumers start associating the visual language of the market leaders with the total product group.

A clear example is the red colour used on the labels of most cola-flavoured beverages. This was originally the colour of the Coca-Cola brand. However, after so many years of Coca-Cola's success, consumers associate the red colour with cola flavour.

Unsurprisingly, the success of Heinz ketchup in the octagonal bottle influenced other producers of ketchup. The degree of resemblance varies from brand to brand.

It is difficult to assess whether the competitors are violating copyright, or just keeping up with consumer expectations for the category. The market leader may not necessarily consider it a disadvantage to have many 'followers'. Perhaps their behaviour only acknowledges the authenticity of the original.

where does the pickle
come from?

THE HEINZ
COMPANY
PRESENTED ITS
WARES WITH A
VERY IMPRESSIVE
EXHIBITION
STAND AT THE
1893 WORLD FAIR
IN CHICAGO.

However, very few visitors were actually
showing up. The stand was 44 steps up the
gallery, which discouraged most potential
passers-by. The founder came up with
a great idea. People were offered a free
individual souvenir if they climbed the stairs
to see the Heinz stand. This was a green
plaster watch charm in the shape of a pickle,
with a metal loop at the top.

It was commonly known as the Heinz Pickle Pin. One million
pins were given away in Chicago. The Pickle Pin was used as a
promotional item for many years. More than 100 million were
handed out at expositions, trade fairs and plant tours, making
it one of the most popular souvenirs in the history of American
advertising. By 1897, the company had officially resolved to use
the pickle bearing the word 'Heinz's' as its logo in all signs, labels,
advertising. The Heinz pickle was more widely known than the
company's trademark. By 1906, however, the pickle logo was no
longer used as the main logo on the labels. It was relegated to a
secondary role, comparable to the old keystone trademark that it had
replaced.

THE 'PICKLE
BRANDED' BOTTLE
FROM 1895

ESTABLISHED 1869

HEINZ

TOMATO
KETCHUP

"QUALITY IS TO A PRODUCT WHAT CHARACTER IS TO A MAN."

HENRY JOHN HEINZ

the magic number 57

THE NECKBAND
AROUND THE HEINZ
KETCHUP BOTTLE
DISPLAYED THE
MAGIC NUMBER '57'
SINCE THE EARLY
TWENTIETH CENTURY

In 1892, the idea of the 57 varieties came to life when Henry John Heinz was riding in a train in New York. He was fascinated by an advertisement in the coach, promoting 21 styles of shoes. He liked how the ad expressed the high number of choices. At the time, he was already manufacturing more than 60 products. However, he kept thinking about the number '57' and '57' varieties, since he considered '57' to be a lucky number. Legend has it that the number '5' was his personal lucky number and '7' was his wife's lucky number.

Besides its presence on the label, the number '57' was also incorporated into the glass of the bottle. According to the Heinz website, a firm tap to this sweet spot on the neck of the bottle will allow the ketchup to be released from the bottle more quickly. It seems that only 11% of people know this secret.

OVER THE YEARS, '57 VARIETIES' HAS BECOME A SLOGAN, COMMUNICATING THE WIDE RANGE SOLD BY THE BRAND. IT HAS NEVER REPRESENTED THE EXACT NUMBER OF PRODUCTS CARRIED BY THE COMPANY.

With Fruit of This Character

—with Heinz pure spices—with only the purest table vinegar of Heinz own make—with refined granulated sugar and condimental seasoning—with preparation in model, clean, open-to-the-public kitchens, can there be any wonder at its rich, home-like flavor and purity, and that

HEINZ
Tomato Ketchup
Needs No Benzoate of Soda

other drugs or artificial preservatives to make it keep? All Heinz 57 Varieties are pure.

The law requires the presence of Benzoate of Soda in Foods to be stated on the label. Read all food labels carefully.

Some of the other seasonable Heinz delicacies are Chili Sauce, Sweet Pickles, Mince Meat, Cranberry Sauce, Apple Butter, Fruit Preserves, Cream of Tomato Soup, etc.

H. J. HEINZ COMPANY

New York   Pittsburgh   Chicago   London

Members of American Association for the Promotion of Purity in Food Products.

free of artificial additives

THE DESIGN OF THE
HEINZ KETCHUP
BOTTLE SHOWED ITS
MOST ICONIC DESIGN
ARCHITECTURE FOR
THE FIRST TIME IN
1890.

Essential features of the iconic design:
The white keystone-shaped label,
emphasized by the gold and green
border. The Heinz logo in black capitals
on the curved baseline and placed
in the shape of the upper part of the
label. Right in the heart of the label, the
product descriptor 'TOMATO KETCHUP'.
The space below the descriptor is dominated by the Heinz pickle
logo and followed by legal information, e.g. production location.
A short white neckband adds the finishing touch.

An additional neck label was introduced in 1906. Its main
message is 'free from benzoate of soda, other drugs, or artificial
preservatives'. Today's consumers might think it looks strange
to have such an unappetizing text on food packaging, even
when the text tries to assure the consumer of the product's
natural contents. For consumers in the early 20th century, it was
very relevant information. Due to the lack of strict legislation,
several manufacturers of ketchup had taken the liberty of putting
suspicious additives in their products. Dyes and chemicals such as
formaldehyde were added to improve flavour, colour and storage
life. Some even used sawdust as a filler. One of the possible
additives was sodium benzoate. The chief chemist for the US
Department of Agriculture, Harvey W. Wiley, challenged the safety of
benzoate. Wiley was supported in particular by Henry J. Heinz, who
opposed to adding chemicals to his products. H.J. Heinz was also
one of the very few food manufacturers at the time who strongly
pushed the new Pure Food and Drug Act of 1906. He believed the
new law would help build consumer confidence in processed food.

Heinz created a new recipe for ketchup that made benzoate
unnecessary. This new recipe is still in use today. The big design
change of 1906 also helped to communicate a change in product to
the consumers.

THE FAVORITE KETCHUP
of 110 nations!

Hands grasp and tilt this appetite-enticing bottle at dining tables up and down the world. Foods of every nation, flecked with Heinz Tomato Ketchup, gain lively flavor—flavor keen with the tangy goodness of vine-fresh, sun-ripened tomatoes, choice spices and other rare good things. Flavor that enriches the enjoyment of almost any food it touches. Flavor that delights the taste of folks in Boston and in Bombay and clear around the world. It's by far the largest-selling ketchup. Is it on your table?

ONE OF THE 57

IN THE FIRST HALF OF THE TWENTIETH CENTURY, THE HEINZ KETCHUP BOTTLE OF 1890 CONQUERED THE WORLD.

In 1948, a bottle design was introduced which is still in use. Compared to the 1890 design, it kept its overall shape, but showed important changes in detailing. In particular, the sharp edges of the octagon shape were smoothed out, and the bottom had a more tapered angle. Overall, the new model looked much more user-friendly and food-appropriate. It also had a better feel in the hand. The label was changed too. It was simplified and lost its Art Nouveau-style drop lines. This design remained almost entirely unchanged for 45 years.

In 2000, the shape and graphics were updated. This time, the changes marked an evolution, rather than a revolution. The keystone label shape was changed slightly to enable faster production. And a new neck label was added with the immortal slogan 'Heinz 57 varieties'.

TOMATO KETCHUP DOMATE
KETCHUP TOMATEAREKIN
TOMATENKETCHUP KET UP
KETCHUP AUX TOMATES
SÒS TOMAT TOMAT
TRÁTAÍ TÓMATSÓSUR
PARADAJZ KEČAP TOM
KEČUPĄ SOS TOMATO
TOMATENKETCHUP
KETCHUP KETCHUP
KEČUP PARADIŽNIKOV
KETCHUP TOMATO
DOMATES KETÇAP
SOS COCH
TOMATO KETCHUP
POMIDOR
TOMATEAREKIN
TOMATKETCHUP
KET UP
KETCHUP AUX
DE TOMATE SÒS
KETCHUP KETCHUP
SAUS TOMAT
KEČAP TOM ĀTU
KEČUPĄ SOS
TAT-TADAM
TOMATKETCHUP
DE TOMATE

KETCHUP POMIDOR KETÇUP
QUETXUP TOMATKETCHUP
TOMAATTIKETSUPPI
KETCHUP DE TOMATE
KETCHUP KETCHUP
SAUS TOMAT KETCHUP
ĀTU KEČUPS POMIDORŲ
KETCHUP TAT-TADAM
TOMATKETCHUP
DE TOMATE KETCHUP
KETCHUP NYANYA
CATSUP KEČUP
CÀ CHUA KETCHUP
TOMATKETCHUP
DOMATE KETCHUP
KETÇUP KETCHUP
QUETXUP
TOMATENKETCHUP
TOMAATTIKETSUPPI
TOMATES KETCHUP
TOMAT TOMAT
TRÁTAÍ TÓMATSÓSUR
KETCHUP PARADAJZ
KEČUPS POMIDORŲ
TOMATO KETCHUP
TOMATENKETCHUP
KETCHUP KETCHUP
KETCHUP KEČUP

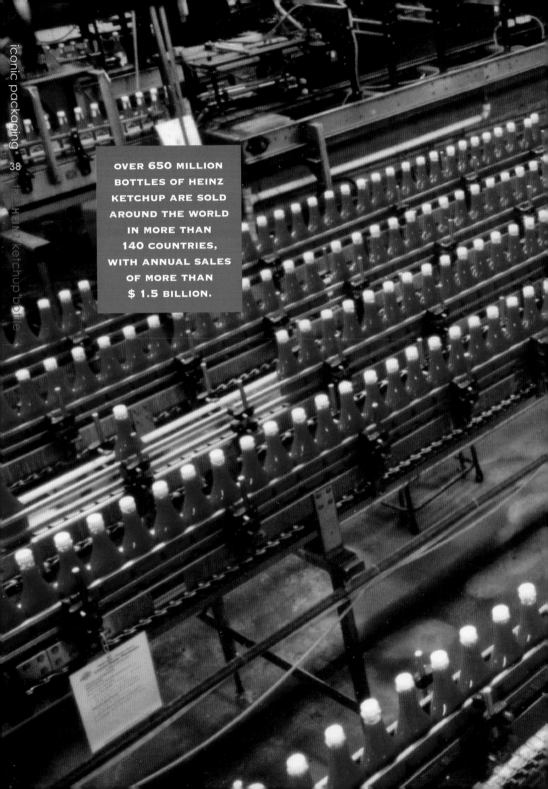

OVER 650 MILLION BOTTLES OF HEINZ KETCHUP ARE SOLD AROUND THE WORLD IN MORE THAN 140 COUNTRIES, WITH ANNUAL SALES OF MORE THAN $ 1.5 BILLION.

the plastic bottle

ICONIC OR NOT, IS
THE OCTAGONAL
GLASS BOTTLE
REALLY USER
FRIENDLY? MANY
HEINZ KETCHUP
LOVERS STILL WANT
'THE REAL THING' IN
'THE REAL BOTTLE'.

Many others prefer the convenience of plastic. Although the plastic bottle seems to be a logical addition to the product range, it took the Heinz company 15 years to develop a bottle that had the right properties. The ketchup is literally boiling hot when it is put in the bottles, so the plastic has to be heat resistant. In addition, the flavour of the ketchup has to remain unaffected by the plastic.

The main question for the company was customer acceptance. When the plastic bottle was introduced, Heinz ketchup faced fierce competition, making it especially important to avoid any image damage. The Heinz team worked with the American Can company for three years before the new bottle was finally introduced. It was only considered ready for its official launch after unbranded home-use tests. Benefits: it was lightweight and scatterproof. The new, convenient, non-removable flip-top cap gave customers better access and portion control.

The new bottle had a very different shape from the octagonal glass bottle. An octagonal shape in plastic wouldn't be easy to squeeze. However, the detailing does reflect its links to its glass ancestor. A fully recyclable plastic bottle was introduced in 1990. At that time, plastic bottles accounted for 60% of the total bottle production.

1983

the first squeezable bottle

IN 2008 A NEW
TRANSPARENT PET
BOTTLE WAS INTRO-
DUCED. THIS BOTTLE
IS SO BRILLIANTLY
CLEAR THAT THE
PURE TOMATO
KETCHUP IS MUCH
MORE VISIBLE. THIS
IS FULLY IN LINE
WITH THE PHILOSO-
PHY OF THE COM-
PANY. IN THE LATE
19TH CENTURY,
H.J. HEINZ HAD SUCH
CONFIDENCE IN THE
QUALITY OF HIS
PRODUCT THAT HE
BECAME THE FIRST
PRODUCER WHO
DARED TO PRESENT
HIS PRODUCTS IN
GLASS. IT WAS A
SIGN OF TRANSPAR-
ENCY AND HONESTY.

strengthening the icon

ONE OF THE KEY FACTORS IN THE GLOBAL FAME OF HEINZ KETCHUP IS THE CONSISTENT USE OF THE KEYSTONE LABEL SHAPE ON ALL HEINZ PRODUCTS.

The repetition of a strong visual element on packaging strengthens the products' impact on the supermarket shelf. At the same time, this repetition helps to build the authority of the brand and embeds it firmly in the visual memory of consumers. There are few examples of brands using their main visual device so consistently over so many years as Heinz.

Since Heinz adheres to extremely strict standards, there was a risk that the brand could be perceived by consumers as hide-bound and old-fashioned. Relying on the strong recognition of the keystone shape, Heinz made allowances for creative freedom on various products that needed more specific category codes, or wanted to address more specific target groups such as children or young mothers.

SOMETIMES EVEN COMMUNICATING WITH A WINK HELPS KEEP THE BRAND ALIVE AND MAINTAINS CONTEMPORARY RELEVANCE.

—hot dogs are *grand!* Tender, toothsome, culent! But did you ever try one with a few f Heinz Tomato Ketchup? Man—there's Racy. Zippy. Sort of *devil-may-care-ish.* mmm . . .

Eats" are in store wherever you see the Tomato Ketchup bottle. For here is the most flavor in the world. From Boston to Bom-inz Tomato Ketchup makes foods *sing*—trans-even ordinary dishes into chefs' triumphs! Tomato Ketchup is so rich and full-bodied much further. But economy is just *one* of

the reasons for the tremendous popularity of this condiment. Heinz Ketchup has a rare old-fashioned flavor that's never successfully imitated! For it's made from Heinz "aristocrat" tomatoes—vine-ripened beauties bred from pedigreed seedlings and *exclusively* controlled by Heinz! With them Heinz cooks skillfully, carefully blend purest granulated sugar, aged-in-wood vinegar and the world's finest spices!

If you're dining out, look for the Heinz Tomato Ketchup bottle. It's a sure sign of "good eats", just as it is on your own table!

advertising

INSPIRING ADVERTISING AND MARKETING HAVE BEEN A PART OF HEINZ'S DNA SINCE THE EARLY DAYS OF THE COMPANY.

Clever advertising can take care of most of the aspects a producer wants to communicate about a branded product. When an effective approach is used, visualizations of applications, ingredients or target groups do not necessarily have to be included on the label to explain the contents.

The packaging can truly remain itself and doesn't need to advertise its contents. This creates a design with iconic potential. Familiarity with the design, and therefore the actual 'iconization', can be particularly enhanced by its recurrent presentation in advertisements.

In fact, the communications from years of promotional efforts are integrated into the iconic bottle's image.

THESE EXAMPLES PROVE
THAT HARDLY ANY
WORDS ARE NEEDED TO
CONVEY THE MESSAGE TO
CONSUMERS. IT BECOMES
ALMOST POETIC.

No one grows Ketchup like Heinz.

The theme was used in various versions, including the immortal 'The slowest ketchup in the west' by Doyle Dane Bernbach. In a saloon full of living ketchup bottles, a 'bad guy' ketchup bottle enters and starts challenging the Heinz ketchup bottle. Heinz wins, while the bad bottle runs empty much faster.

dipping and squeezing

SINCE 1968, THE
GLASS AND PLASTIC
KETCHUP BOTTLES
HAVE FACED STRONG
COMPETITION
FROM WITHIN THE
COMPANY: THE
PORTION PACKS.

These packs show an illustration of the octagon bottle as an identification of the product's authenticity and quality. Heinz currently sells so many packs that, if they were lined up, they would stretch all the way to the moon and back, and even further. Despite its success, there was still room for innovation.

A more convenient packaging solution could be a hit, especially among users 'on the go'. Not only would it cut down on concerns of creating a mess, it would also offer consumers more flexibility. The Heinz Dip & Squeeze™ is designed with a dual functionality. One end can be torn off, so the ketchup can be squeezed out and used as a topping. The foil on the other end can be pulled back to create a dipping container for fries. It holds more than three times the amount of the traditional portion packet.

The 2010 introduction of the new packs was planned to take place at select fast-food restaurants in the USA. Recognition is assured with the good old octagonal bottle image.

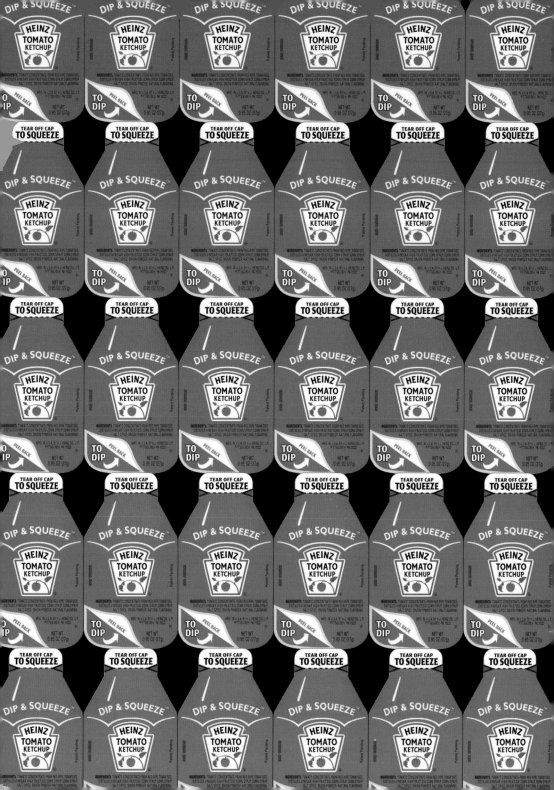

talking labels

THE HEINZ'S 'TALKING LABELS' PROGRAMME WAS LAUNCHED IN THE USA IN 1999. USING THE 'UNTOUCHABLE' LABEL AS A PROMOTIONAL PLATFORM WAS SEEN AS A DARING STEP.

Initially, the company wanted to boost consumption among teens and households with kids, resulting in the 'Ketchup with Attitude' strategy. The kick-off was the 'talking labels' programme, in which unorthodox and quirky sayings were put on the Heinz ketchup labels for a limited time.

Following from this successful strategy, an extension was launched to celebrate the company's 130th anniversary. Visitors to the MyHeinz website could create their own custom printed labels. People could choose from three bottle types, create a message, pay for the order and have it shipped instantly. It was a smash hit, and several follow-ups were developed over the years. One example is the 2002 'Say Something Ketchuppy' summer contest. Consumers were able to submit their own 'talking label' ideas to Heinz. Heinz's 'talking labels' even inspired some other big food brands to run similar promotions.

THE WINNING
PHRASES INCLUDED:
• BETTER LOOKING
THAN RELISH
• COMFORTS BURNT
HOT DOGS
• WARNING: SLOW
MOVING CONDIMENT

HEINZ

ESTᴰ 1869 ESTᴰ

WHAT WILL
YOU SAY?

WWW.MYHEINZ.COM

HEINZ Ⓤ

America's Favorite Ketchup™

NET WT 14 OZ-397 GRAMS

H.J. HEINZ CO.

HEINZ

ESTᴰ 1869 ESTᴰ

SAY IT IN A
BIG WAY

NET WT 2.25 OZ-64g

limited editions

ONE OF HEINZ'S MOST SPECTACULAR
SERIES OF LIMITED EDITIONS WAS
THE JEWELLED CELEBRITY
'TALKING LABEL' BOTTLES
WITH THOUSANDS OF TINY RED
SWAROVSKI CRYSTALS.

These bottles were issued in 2004 for the
'Heinz Pours it On for Charity' auction at
Sotheby's in New York. Each label had
a 'ketchup quote' from movie stars or
sports heroes, including Lindsay Lohan,
William Shatner, Mia Hamm and Terry
Bradshaw.

The jewels were applied by hand by Los
Angeles artist Scott Devlin, who used
5102 tiny Swarovski crystals for the
finished product.

A far more accessible limited
edition ketchup bottle
was introduced in 2009
for the company's 140th
anniversary, celebrating
the first design of the
octagonal bottle with the
keystone label.

GEF7538

THIS CUSTOM HEINZ
KETCHUP DUNNY
WAS MADE BY
CONNECTICUT-BASED
GRAFFITI ARTIST
SKET ONE.

ketchup dunny and
ketchupsaurus

DUNNIES ARE AMONG THE MOST POPULAR AND BEST KNOWN DESIGNER TOYS AROUND, PRODUCED BY THE KIDROBOT COMPANY.

Sket One's dunny is part of a series, all on the theme of famous condiments and drinks. He loves pop art objects from his own past. The message he tries to convey is that cool stuff is being designed every day by designers who study and explore design, and the end result is as simple as mustard and ketchup packages. While the designer toys were initially limited runs, providing a canvas for the 'anti-commercial' work, mainly created by street artists and graffiti artists, they have now become mass-produced supermarket products themselves.

Ketchupsaurus (by Kristine Martinez) was made in 2004 for the DinoMite days in the city of Pittsburgh. It was sponsored by the H.J. Heinz Corporation and exhibited in the open air for four months, along with 99 more creations by dinosaur-inspired artists. These have been auctioned off to raise money for the Carnegie Museum of Natural History.

© photo Ed Lehman, San Diego

the ketchup creativity contest

THE WINNERS WILL HAVE THEIR DESIGNS PRINTED ON ALMOST 20 MILLION HEINZ KETCHUP PORTION PACKETS.

The Ketchup Creativity Contest is the name of a nationwide ketchup packet design competition for students in primary and secondary schools across the US, challenging the artistic skills of these aspiring young artists.

This annual competition organized by Heinz Food Service was first held in 2006. A panel of judges selects the top three entries in each grade. These artworks are then published online so the public can vote for their favourites. In addition to the contest, the initiative includes an educational resource for teachers, promoting the benefits of eating nutritious foods.

art for charity

WHEN IT'S YOUR BIRTHDAY, IT'S YOUR TURN TO HAND OUT THE TREATS. THIS IS A COMMON CUSTOM IN THE NETHERLANDS.

To celebrate its 140th anniversary in 2009, Heinz Netherlands decided to get involved in the Fight Cancer program, the youth chapter of the KWF Dutch Cancer Society. Famous Dutch DJ and artist Ruud de Wild was asked to create a work of art on the theme of Heinz ketchup. Once it was finished, the artwork travelled around the country in a specially designed mobile showcase, drawing attention to the objectives of Fight Cancer. The painting was finally raffled off among the people who had contributed by giving a donation to Fight Cancer.

Ruud de Wild took part in the project without financial compensation. He was free to choose any subject related to Heinz ketchup, and chose the original Keystone label as his starting point. The style and palette he used was inspired by the visual language of the circus, which travels around just like the painting.

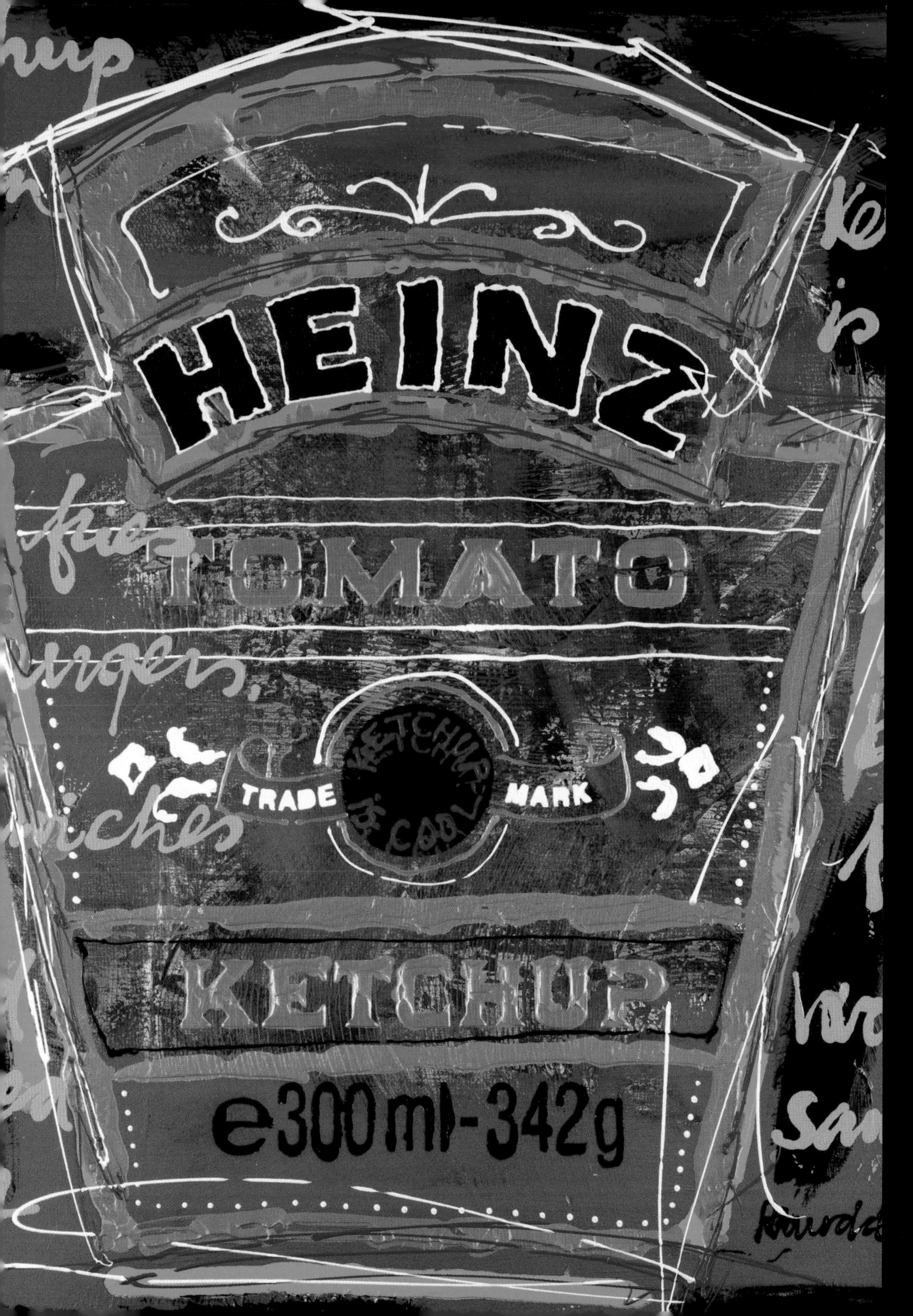
HEINZ
TOMATO
TRADE
MARK
KETCHUP
e300ml-342g

czech art

These pages show the fascinating results of a competition initiated by the Czech Heinz company, celebrating its 140th anniversary. The company's appreciation of modern and iconic design goes back to its early days. The value of Heinz's iconic design was also recognized by the Prague University of Art, which started a project in cooperation with Heinz. Students were asked to present their perspective on the future of Heinz products by developing creative work. The many proposals included various highly interesting interpretations of the ketchup bottle.

Yveta Kroupová,
Bottle with 12 tomatoes

Orla Walsh,
Donut Ketchup

author's note

bibliography

First of all, I'd like to thank Menno van der Vlist of H.J. Heinz Company Netherlands, who has been a great supporter of this book. He has spent many hours checking the content of my pages and provided lots of artwork.

I would also like to thank Ed Lehew of H.J. Heinz Company USA, who dug into the archives to find the answers to my toughest questions.
Ed also provided me with beautiful photos and original labels. I see both Menno and Ed as my most important sources. My last words of thanks go to the Heinz Corporate Affairs department, Imo Muller, Sket One, Ruud de Wild, Kristýna Smitková, Barbara Starostová and many others.

Coolbrands *the Guru Book.*
Cool Unlimited.
CoolbrandsHouse 2007
Pure Ketchup *A history of America's national condiment.*
Andrew F. Smith.
The Smithsonian Institute: 2001.
In good company *125 years at the Heinz table.* Eleanor Foa Dienstag.
The H.J. Heinz Company: 1994.
How it all began *The stories behind those famous names.* Maurice Baren. Smith Settle Ltd.: 1992.
The Art of the Label Robert Opie. Chartwell Books Inc.: 1987.

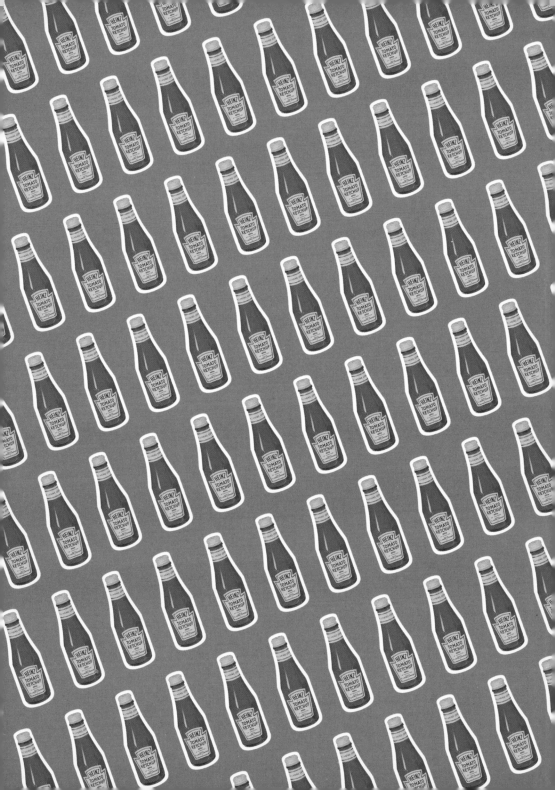